Planters

Connor Dayton

PowerKiDS press.

New York

Published in 2012 by The Rosen Publishing Group, Inc.
29 East 21st Street, New York, NY 10010

First Edition

Editor: Jennifer Way
Book Design: Greg Tucker

Photo Credits: Cover © Wayne Hutchinson/age fotostock; pp. 4–5, 7, 9, 10–11, 12–13, 18–19, 23, 24 (top left, bottom left, bottom right) Shutterstock.com; p. 15 Scott Olson/Getty Images; pp. 17, 24 (top right) Mark Hirsch/Bloomberg via Getty Images; p. 21 PhotoAlto/Laurence Mouton/Getty Images.

Library of Congress Cataloging-in-Publication Data

Dayton, Connor.
 Planters / by Connor Dayton. — 1st ed.
    p. cm. — (Farm machines)
 Includes index.
 ISBN 978-1-4488-4947-5 (library binding) — ISBN 978-1-4488-5044-0 (pbk.) —
ISBN 978-1-4488-5045-7 (6-pack)
1. Planters (Agricultural machinery)—Juvenile literature. I. Title.
TJ1483.D39 2012
631.3'7—dc22

                          2010048104

Manufactured in the United States of America

CPSIA Compliance Information: Batch #WS11PK: For Further Information contact Rosen Publishing, New York, New York at 1-800-237-9932

Contents

Farmers use planters
in their **fields**.

Tractors pull planters into the fields. The hitch joins the planter to the tractor.

Planters put seeds into fields. Planting seeds is called sowing.

Some planters sow corn. Most American corn is grown in Iowa.

Planters sow many rows at once. The rows must be evenly spaced.

Seeds must be evenly spaced in each row. This is the planter's job.

Planters come in different sizes. Big planters have many **row units**.

Each row unit sows
one row.

The seeds go through the row unit. Then they go into the ground.

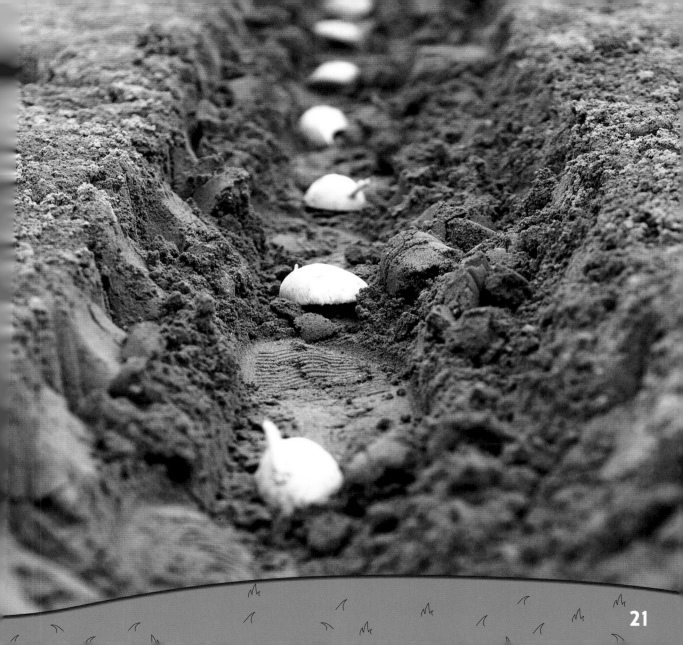

Soon the seeds will **sprout**. The new crops fill the field.

Words to Know

field

row units

sprout

tractor

Index

Web Sites

Due to the changing nature of Internet links, PowerKids Press has developed an online list of Web sites related to the subject of this book. This site is updated regularly. Please use this link to access the list:
www.powerkidslinks.com/farm/planters/